HOW TO BECOME THE BOSS OF YOUR EMOTIONS

The Ultimate Guide To Have A Great Mental Health

VOL 1

Dennys Volkovski

Contents

Introduction

Emotional health is an essential component of overall health and well-being. It refers to the ability of an individual to effectively manage, understand, and express their emotions in a healthy and adaptive manner. Good emotional health is characterized by a sense of emotional balance, resilience, positive relationships, and the ability to cope with stress and adversity. On the other hand, poor emotional health can result in emotional dysregulation, stress, anxiety, and a host of other mental health issues.

In today's fast-paced and demanding world, maintaining emotional health is becoming increasingly important. Many individuals are struggling with managing their emotions, leading to decreased overall well-being and increased levels of stress. However, emotional health is not a fixed state and can be improved through various practices and habits. By investing in emotional health, individuals can not only improve their overall quality of life but also their ability to handle life's challenges with resilience and grace.

In this guide, we will explore what emotional health is, why it is important, and various techniques and practices that individuals can use to improve their emotional health. Whether you are looking to gain a better understanding of your emotions, manage negative emotions, cultivate positive emotions, or simply improve your overall emotional health, this guide will provide you with the tools and information you need to be the boss of your emotions.

Definition of Emotional Health

Emotional health refers to an individual's ability to effectively understand, manage, and express their emotions in a healthy and adaptive manner. It encompasses a range of psychological and social factors that contribute to an individual's overall well-being, such as self-awareness, resilience, positive relationships, and the ability to cope with stress and adversity. Good emotional health allows individuals to experience a full range of emotions without letting them interfere with their daily functioning, relationships, or sense of self-worth. In contrast, poor emotional health can lead to emotional deregulation, stress, anxiety, depression, and a host of other mental health issues. Emotional health is an important aspect of overall health and can be developed and maintained through various practices, such as mindfulness, self-care, and seeking support from others.

Moreover, emotional health is closely linked to physical health, as chronic stress and negative emotions can have negative impacts on the body, such as decreased immunity, increased risk of chronic illness, and decreased overall physical functioning.

On the other hand, positive emotions and emotional regulation have been shown to have positive impacts on physical health, such as improved immune function, reduced risk of chronic illness, and improved overall physical functioning.

Emotional health is not a fixed state and can change over time based on various life experiences, events, and stressors. It is a dynamic and ongoing process of growth and development, and it is never too late to start working on improving one's emotional health. By developing a strong emotional foundation, individuals can not only increase their overall well-being but also their ability to handle life's challenges with resilience and grace. Emotional health is an important aspect of overall health and well-being that contributes to an individual's ability to effectively manage their emotions, build positive relationships, and cope with stress and adversity. By investing in emotional health, individuals can improve their overall quality of life and increase their resilience to life's challenges.

Importance Of Emotional Mastery

Emotional mastery is the ability to understand, manage, and regulate one's emotions, thoughts, and behaviors in a healthy and productive manner. It involves recognizing emotions as they arise, examining the underlying causes of those emotions, and taking steps to manage them in a way that supports our well-being and goals

Why Is It Important To Be The Boss Of Your Emotions?

It is important to be the boss of your emotions for several reasons:

- Improved mental health: Being the boss of your emotions means being able to effectively manage and regulate your emotions, reducing the negative impact that stress and emotional dysregulation can have on mental health.

- Improved relationships: When you are the boss of your emotions, you are better able to manage conflicts, communicate effectively, and build stronger, more fulfilling relationships with others.

- Increased resilience: Being able to regulate your emotions and manage stress effectively means you are better equipped to handle life's challenges with resilience and grace.

- Enhanced personal growth: When you are in control of your emotions, you are better able to understand yourself, identify areas for growth, and pursue your goals and aspirations.

- Improved physical health: Emotional health and physical health are closely linked. When you are the boss of your emotions, you are better able to manage stress and negative emotions, which can have positive impacts on physical health, such as improved immunity, reduced risk of chronic illness, and improved overall physical functioning.

- Increased confidence and self-esteem: When you are able to effectively manage your emotions, you are more confident in your abilities and feel a greater sense of self-worth. This can lead to increased success in both personal and professional areas of life.
- Improved decision-making: Being in control of your emotions means being able to make decisions based on reason and logic rather than being driven by emotional impulses. This can lead to more thoughtful, well-informed decisions that are in line with your values and goals.
- Greater happiness and overall life satisfaction: When you are the boss of your emotions, you are better able to experience a full range of emotions without letting them interfere with your daily functioning or sense of self-worth. This can lead to greater happiness and overall life satisfaction.
- Better coping skills: Being the boss of your emotions means being able to effectively manage stress and adversity, this can increase your overall coping skills and ability to handle life's challenges.
- A sense of control: When you are the boss of your emotions, you are better able to understand and control your emotional responses, giving you a greater sense of control over your life and reducing feelings of helplessness or frustration.

Being the boss of your emotions is important because it can lead to improved mental and physical health, better relationships, increased resilience, and personal growth. By investing in emotional health, individuals can lead a happier, more fulfilling life.

Benefits OF A HEALTHY MENTAL STATE

A healthy mental state refers to a state of well-being characterized by positive emotions, clear thinking, and effective functioning. There are many benefits to having a healthy mental state, including:

- Increased Happiness: When our mental state is healthy, we experience a greater sense of happiness, fulfillment, and contentment.
- Improved Relationships: A healthy mental state enables us to communicate effectively and build stronger relationships with others.
- Enhanced Performance: People with a healthy mental state are better able to concentrate, problem-solve, and perform at a higher level in work and other areas of life.
- Increased Resilience: A healthy mental state helps us to better cope with stress and adversity, leading to increased resilience and a more positive outlook on life.
- Better Physical Health: Mental health and physical health are closely related, and a healthy mental state can have a positive impact on physical health, reducing the risk of many chronic health conditions.
- Increased Creativity: A healthy mental state can also lead to increased creativity and the ability to see new solutions to problems.
- Improved Self-Esteem: When our mental state is healthy, we feel more confident, positive, and self-assured, leading to an improved self-esteem.

In conclusion, maintaining a healthy mental state has numerous benefits, ranging from increased happiness and better relationships, to enhanced performance and improved physical health. By prioritizing our mental health and well-being, we can live a happier, more fulfilling life.

Understanding The Connection Between Thoughts, Feelings and Behaviors

Understanding the connection between thoughts, feelings and behaviors is a critical aspect of emotional intelligence and mental health. Our thoughts, feelings, and behaviors are all interconnected and influence one another in a continuous feedback loop. In order to maintain good mental health and well-being, it is essential to understand this connection and how to manage it effectively. Thoughts, feelings, and behaviors are all integral components of our mental and emotional experiences. Our thoughts can be described as the ideas, beliefs, and judgments that we have about ourselves, others, and the world around us. Thoughts can be conscious or unconscious and can be influenced by our past experiences, cultural upbringing, and current circumstances. Feelings are emotional responses to our thoughts and experiences. They are the sensations we experience in our bodies when we think about something or encounter a particular situation. Feelings can range from positive emotions such as joy and love to negative emotions such as sadness and anger. Behaviors are the actions we take in response to our thoughts and feelings. They can be conscious or unconscious and can range from physical actions such as smiling or crying to more complex actions such as speaking or writing. Behaviors can be influenced by our thoughts, feelings, and the environment we find ourselves in.

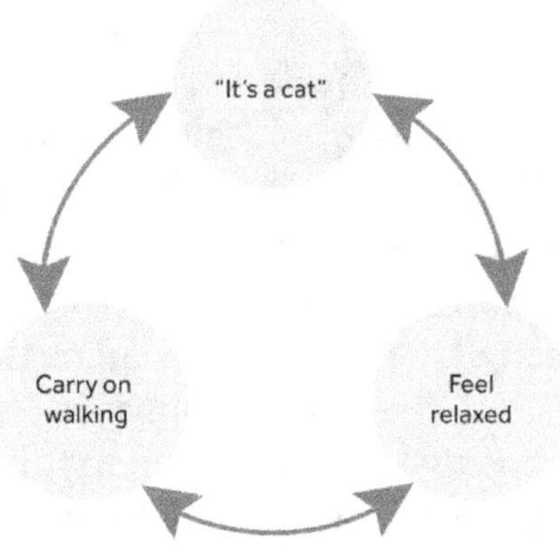

The connection between thoughts, feelings, and behaviors is a continuous feedback loop. Our thoughts influence our feelings, which in turn influence our behaviors, and our behaviors can then influence our thoughts and feelings. For example, if someone has a negative thought about themselves such as "I am not good enough," this thought can trigger feelings of sadness, anxiety, or low self-esteem. These feelings can then lead to behaviors such as avoiding social situations, procrastination, or self-criticism.

These behaviors can then reinforce the negative thought, creating a vicious cycle. Conversely, if someone has a positive thought such as "I am capable and competent," this thought can trigger feelings of confidence and self-esteem. These feelings can then lead to behaviors such as seeking new challenges, taking risks, and pursuing goals. These behaviors can then reinforce the positive thought, creating a virtuous cycle.

In order to maintain good mental health, it is important to understand this connection and learn how to manage it effectively. One way to do this is by developing mindfulness, which is the practice of being present and aware of our thoughts, feelings, and behaviors. Mindfulness allows us to observe our thoughts, feelings, and behaviors without judgment, which can help us understand the connection between them and make changes as necessary.

Another way to manage the connection between thoughts, feelings, and behaviors is to practice positive self-talk. Positive self-talk is the practice of speaking kindly and compassionately to ourselves. It involves replacing negative thoughts with positive ones and reminding ourselves of our strengths and abilities. This can help to increase feelings of self-esteem and confidence, which can lead to positive behaviors. Exercise and physical activity can also play a role in managing the connection between thoughts, feelings, and behaviors. Exercise has been shown to have a positive impact on mental health by reducing stress and anxiety, improving mood, and increasing self-esteem.

Regular physical activity can also help to regulate our emotions and reduce the intensity of negative feelings. Good sleep is also important for maintaining the connection between thoughts, feelings, and behaviors. Poor sleep can negatively impact our mental health by increasing stress and anxiety, reducing mood, and impacting our ability to think clearly. On the other hand, good sleep can help us to regulate our emotions, reduce stress, and improve our overall well-being.

Finally, it is important to seek support from friends, family, or mental health professionals when necessary.

The Connection Between Diet and Mental Health

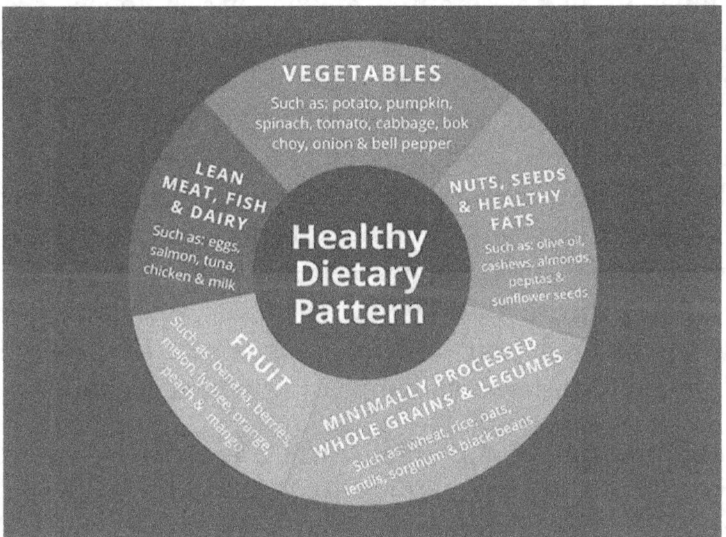

The connection between diet and mental health is a growing field of study that is increasingly being recognized as important. Research has shown that the food we eat can have a significant impact on our mental health and well-being, including our mood, behavior, and cognitive function. In this article, we will explore the connection between diet and mental health, and how making healthy food choices can improve our overall mental health.

One of the most significant ways that diet can impact mental health is through the effects of certain nutrients on neurotransmitter function. Neurotransmitters are chemical messengers in the brain that are responsible for transmitting signals between nerve cells. They play a critical role in regulating mood, behavior, and cognitive function. The type and amount of nutrients that we consume can impact the production and function of neurotransmitters, and therefore, have a significant impact on our mental health. For example, low levels of B vitamins, such as folate and vitamin B12, have been linked to an increased risk of depression. Omega-3 fatty acids, which are found in foods such as fatty fish and flaxseeds, have been shown to be beneficial for mental health, as they play a role in regulating neurotransmitter function and reducing inflammation in the brain. Antioxidant-rich foods, such as berries, leafy greens, and nuts, can also improve mental health by protecting the brain from oxidative stress and promoting healthy brain function. Another important factor in the connection between diet and mental health is blood sugar regulation. Consuming a diet that is high in sugar and refined carbohydrates can lead to rapid fluctuations in blood sugar levels, which can impact mood, behavior, and cognitive function. This is why a diet that is rich in whole foods, such as vegetables, whole grains, and lean protein, is beneficial for maintaining stable blood sugar levels and improving mental health.

Gut health is also an important consideration in the connection between diet and mental health. The gut and brain are connected by the gut-brain axis, and a healthy gut microbiome can impact mental health by producing neurotransmitters, regulating immune function, and reducing inflammation.

A diet that is high in fermented foods, such as yogurt, kefir, and sauerkraut, can help to support a healthy gut microbiome and improve mental health. In addition to the specific nutrients and food groups that can impact mental health, the overall quality of the diet is also important. A diet that is high in processed foods, added sugars, and unhealthy fats can increase the risk of depression, anxiety, and other mental health conditions. On the other hand, a diet that is rich in whole, nutrient-dense foods can support mental health by providing the body with the nutrients it needs to function properly and promoting overall well-being. It is also important to consider the social and emotional factors that are associated with eating habits. Eating can be a source of comfort and enjoyment, but it can also be a source of stress and anxiety. For example, restrictive dieting, binge eating, and other disordered eating patterns can have a significant impact on mental health. Finding a healthy balance between nourishing the body and enjoying food can help to support mental health and well-being.

In conclusion, the connection between diet and mental health is a complex and multifaceted relationship. However, it is clear that the food we eat can have a significant impact on our mental health and well-being. By focusing on a diet that is rich in nutrient-dense, whole foods, and limiting processed foods and added sugars, we can support our mental health and improve our overall well-being.

Understanding Emotions

Understanding Emotions is a critical aspect of becoming the boss of your emotions. Emotions are complex and dynamic experiences that can play a major role in our lives. By understanding emotions, individuals can better identify their emotional responses and manage them effectively.

What Are Emotions?

Emotions are complex and subjective experiences that can be triggered by events, thoughts, or other stimuli. Emotions can be experienced as a blend of psychological and physical sensations and can impact our thoughts, behaviors, and overall well-being. Emotions can be positive, such as joy, love, or gratitude, or negative, such as anger, fear, or sadness. They can range in intensity and duration, and can be influenced by various factors, including genetics, personality, life experiences, and cultural influences.

Emotions serve as an important signaling system that provides information about the environment and helps individuals respond to different situations. For example, feelings of joy can signal that something is going well, while feelings of fear can signal that a person is in danger. Emotions are a fundamental aspect of human experience and play a critical role in our lives. By understanding and managing our emotions, we can improve our well-being and build a more fulfilling and satisfying life.

Common Emotions and Their Meanings

There are many emotions that individuals' experience and some of the most common emotions include:

- Joy: A feeling of happiness, satisfaction, and well-being. Joy can be triggered by events, achievements, or other positive experiences.
- Love: A strong feeling of affection and attachment towards someone or something. Love can be experienced as a warm, positive emotion, and can be expressed in many different forms, including romantic love, familial love, and love for pets, hobbies, or other interests.
- Anger: A strong emotion characterized by feelings of annoyance, frustration, and annoyance. Anger can be triggered by perceived injustices, conflicts, or other challenges.
- Fear: A feeling of anxiety, nervousness, or dread in response to a perceived threat. Fear can be experienced as a physical sensation, such as increased heart rate or sweating, and can motivate individuals to take action to protect themselves.
- Sadness: A feeling of disappointment, loss, or despair. Sadness can be triggered by a loss or disappointment,

such as the end of a relationship, the loss of a loved one, or other challenges.

- Guilt: A feeling of responsibility for something that has gone wrong. Guilt can be triggered by a perceived failure, or by a belief that one has done something wrong or unethical.

- Envy: A feeling of resentment or jealousy towards someone who has something that one desires. Envy can be triggered by a comparison with others, or by a desire for what others have.

- Pride: A feeling of satisfaction, self-respect, or accomplishment. Pride can be experienced as a positive emotion and can be triggered by achievements, recognition, or other accomplishments.

In conclusion, emotions can be positive, negative, or a blend of both, and can play a critical role in shaping our thoughts, behaviors, and experiences. By understanding the meaning and function of emotions, individuals can better manage their emotional lives and build a more fulfilling and satisfying life.

Emotional Triggers

Emotional triggers are stimuli that provoke an emotional response. Emotional triggers can range from external events, such as a challenging situation, to internal thoughts and memories. They can evoke a range of emotions, from positive feelings, such as joy and love, to negative emotions, such as fear, anger, and sadness. Emotional triggers can impact an individual's thoughts, behaviors, and overall well-being. Emotional triggers are unique to each individual and can be shaped by a variety of factors, including genetics, life experiences, and cultural influences. For example, an individual who has experienced trauma may have different emotional triggers than someone who has not experienced such events. Similarly, an individual who grew up in an environment with a lot of conflict may have different emotional triggers than someone who grew up in a supportive and nurturing environment. It is important to understand and manage emotional triggers because they can have a significant impact on mental health. For example, if an individual has strong emotional triggers associated with negative experiences, they may experience intense and overwhelming emotions that can disrupt their daily life. On the other hand, if an individual has a better understanding of their emotional triggers, they can learn to regulate their emotional responses and avoid negative emotions from taking over. Understanding and managing emotional triggers is an important aspect of emotional health. By recognizing and learning to cope with their emotional triggers, individuals can improve their emotional well-being; reduce stress, and build a more fulfilling and satisfying life.

Emotional Responses

Emotional responses refer to the ways in which individuals react to and experience emotions. Emotional responses are complex and can vary greatly from person to person, depending on individual experiences, personality, and cultural background.

Emotional responses can range from mild to intense and can be expressed through various forms of behavior, such as facial expressions, body language, or verbal communication. Some common emotional responses include:

- ✓ Crying: Tears can be a natural and instinctive response to emotions such as sadness, grief, or frustration.
- ✓ Laughter: Laughter is a common response to positive emotions such as joy, excitement, or happiness.
- ✓ Anger: Anger is a natural response to perceived threats or injustice, and can be expressed through physical or verbal behaviors.
- ✓ Fear: Fear is an instinctive response to danger or potential harm, and can result in physical symptoms such as increased heart rate or sweating.

✓ Numbness: In response to overwhelming emotions, some individuals may experience a sense of numbness or detachment, as a way of coping.

Emotional responses can be automatic and unconscious, or they can be consciously controlled and managed. It is important to understand our emotional responses and to work towards managing them in a healthy way, as our emotional responses can greatly impact our relationships, decision making, and overall well-being.

Identifying And Managing Negative Emotions

Identifying and managing negative emotions is an essential part of maintaining good emotional health. Negative emotions, such as anger, fear, sadness, and anxiety, can have a profound impact on our well-being and can disrupt our daily life. However, by recognizing and managing these emotions, individuals can improve their mental health and build a more fulfilling and satisfying life. To identify negative emotions, it is important to pay attention to physical sensations, thoughts, and behaviors. For example, an individual may feel tightness in their chest, an increased heart rate, or negative thoughts when they are experiencing negative emotions. By becoming aware of these physical and mental symptoms, individuals can learn to recognize when they are experiencing negative emotions.

Once an individual has identified negative emotions, they can begin to manage them by utilizing coping strategies. There are a variety of coping strategies that can be effective in managing negative emotions, including:

- ✓ Mindfulness: Practicing mindfulness can help individuals become more aware of their thoughts and emotions, and can promote a more relaxed and peaceful state of mind.
- ✓ Exercise: Exercise can help to reduce stress and release endorphins, which can improve mood and reduce negative emotions.
- ✓ Journaling: Writing about one's emotions can help individuals gain clarity and insight into their thoughts and feelings.
- ✓ Relaxation techniques: Relaxation techniques, such as deep breathing, progressive muscle relaxation, and meditation, can help individuals reduce stress and manage negative emotions.
- ✓ Seek support: Talking to a trusted friend or loved one, or seeking support from a mental health professional, can help individuals process and manage negative emotions.

It's also important to note that managing negative emotions is not about suppressing or ignoring them. Negative emotions are a normal and healthy part of the human experience and can serve as valuable signals that something in our lives may need to change. Instead, the goal of managing negative emotions is to regulate them in a healthy way, so they don't become overwhelming or interfere with our daily life.

Additionally, it's important to understand that managing negative emotions can be a long-term process and requires a commitment to self-reflection and self-care. Individuals may need to experiment with different coping strategies to find what works best for them and it may take time and practice to develop effective coping mechanisms. It's also important to be gentle with yourself and to recognize that it's okay to experience negative emotions. Everyone struggles with negative emotions from time to time, and it's important to avoid self-criticism and judgment and to practice self-compassion.

Finally, it's important to seek help when needed. If negative emotions are affecting your daily life and well-being, it may be helpful to seek support from a mental health professional, such as a therapist or counselor. They can provide guidance and support in developing effective coping strategies and improving emotional health.

Common Negative Emotions

Common negative emotions are a normal part of the human experience and can serve as signals that something in our lives may need to change. Negative emotions can range in intensity and frequency and can vary from person to person. Some common negative emotions include anger, fear, sadness, anxiety, guilt, shame, envy, jealousy, and frustration.

Anger is a strong feeling of annoyance, displeasure, or hostility towards someone or something. Fear is an intense feeling of worry or nervousness about a perceived threat or danger. Sadness is a feeling of sorrow or unhappiness often associated with loss or disappointment. Anxiety is a feeling of worry, nervousness, or unease about an event or situation, often without a clear cause. Guilt is a feeling of remorse or self-blame for something one believes they did wrong. Shame is a feeling of humiliation or embarrassment about one's self or actions. Envy is a feeling of resentment or bitterness towards someone else's success or good fortune. Jealousy is a feeling of suspicion or mistrust towards a partner or close friend, often regarding a perceived threat to a relationship. Frustration is a feeling of disappointment or irritation caused by an obstacle to achieving a goal.

Techniques To Identify Negative Emotions

There are several techniques that can help individuals identify and understand their negative emotions:

- Mindfulness: Practicing mindfulness, or being present in the moment, can help individuals identify when negative emotions arise and how they manifest in the body.
- Journaling: Writing down thoughts and feelings can help individuals identify patterns and triggers of negative emotions.

- Body Awareness: Paying attention to physical sensations in the body, such as tightness in the chest or a racing heart, can help individuals identify when negative emotions are present.
- Reflection: Taking time to reflect on the events and situations that led to the negative emotion can help individuals identify the root cause of the emotion.
- Emotion Regulation Strategies: Practicing techniques such as deep breathing, progressive muscle relaxation, and visualization can help individuals regulate their emotions.
- Emotion Word List: Creating a list of words to describe different emotions can help individuals identify and label their emotions more accurately.
- Emotion Rating Scale: Using a numerical rating system, such as 0-10, to rate the intensity of emotions can help individuals track changes in emotional intensity over time.
- Emotion Recognition Software: There are various software programs and smartphone apps that use artificial intelligence to recognize and label emotions based on facial expressions and voice patterns.
- Cognitive Behavioral Therapy (CBT): CBT is a type of therapy that can help individuals identify and challenge negative thoughts and beliefs that contribute to negative emotions.
- Mind-Body Practices: Mind-body practices such as yoga, tai chi, and meditation can help individuals increase awareness of physical sensations and emotions, and develop strategies for regulating emotions.

By regularly using these techniques, individuals can become more aware of their negative emotions and develop strategies for managing them in a healthy way. It's important to remember that everyone's emotional experience is unique and it may take time and practice to develop effective techniques for managing negative emotions.

Techniques To Manage Negative Emotions

Once negative emotions have been identified, there are several techniques that can help individuals manage and regulate them:

- Mindfulness-based techniques: Mindfulness-based techniques, such as deep breathing, meditation, and progressive muscle relaxation, can help individuals regulate their emotions by reducing stress and anxiety.
- Cognitive-behavioral techniques: Cognitive-behavioral techniques such as reframing negative thoughts and challenging negative beliefs can help individuals change their perspective on a situation and reduce negative emotions.
- Problem-solving: Using a structured problem-solving approach can help individuals find practical solutions to the events and situations that trigger negative emotions.
- Emotional expression: Expressing emotions through activities such as journaling, art, or talking to a trusted friend or therapist can help individuals release and regulate negative emotions.
- Physical activity: Engaging in physical activity, such as exercise, yoga, or tai chi, can help individuals reduce stress and regulate emotions by releasing endorphins and reducing muscle tension.
- Self-care: Engaging in self-care activities, such as getting enough sleep, eating a balanced diet, and pursuing hobbies and interests, can help individuals maintain physical and emotional well-being.
- Seeking support: Talking to a trusted friend, family member, or mental health professional can provide support and help individuals develop strategies for managing negative emotions.

It's important to remember that managing negative emotions is a process and it may take time and practice to develop effective techniques. It's also important to seek support from a mental health professional if negative emotions become overwhelming or interfere with daily life. With time, patience, and practice, individuals can learn to regulate their emotions and lead a fulfilling and satisfying life.

Cultivating Positive Emotions

Positive emotions are feelings that are considered pleasurable and enjoyable, such as joy, happiness, love, excitement, and satisfaction. These emotions enhance our sense of well-being and add to our quality of life. Positive emotions broaden our perspective, foster creativity, and improve our relationships with others. Positive emotions also play an important role in physical health by strengthening our immune system and reducing stress levels. Overall, positive emotions are seen as essential for a healthy and fulfilling life, and cultivating them can lead to greater happiness and satisfaction.

Gratitude: A feeling of appreciation and Cultivating positive emotions refers to the intentional process of fostering positive experiences and attitudes in order to enhance one's overall emotional well-being. This can be achieved through various techniques and practices, such as mindfulness, gratitude, positive self-talk, and engaging in meaningful activities. Some other ways to cultivate positive emotions include setting achievable goals, practicing positive habits, building strong and supportive relationships, and celebrating small victories. Practicing kindness and compassion towards oneself and others can also increase feelings of happiness, connection, and purpose. Additionally, incorporating physical activity into one's routine, such as exercise or yoga, can improve both physical and emotional health. Engaging in creative pursuits such as; art or music, can also bring joy and fulfillment. Practicing relaxation techniques, such as deep breathing or meditation, can help reduce stress and improve overall emotional well-being. It's also important to recognize that positive emotions don't always come naturally, and it can be helpful to seek out opportunities to experience them. This can mean trying new experiences, surrounding one with positive people, or engaging in activities that bring joy and happiness.

Another important aspect of cultivating positive emotions is to challenge negative thinking patterns and reframe negative thoughts into more positive ones, for example, instead of focusing on what one cannot do, focus on what one can do, and seek out opportunities to build on strengths and abilities.

Common Positive Emotions

Common positive emotions include:

- ✓ Joy thankfulness for what one has.
- ✓ Hope: A feeling of optimistic expectation or desire for a particular outcome.
- ✓ Pride: A feeling of satisfaction and accomplishment in one's own achievements or those of someone close to them.
- ✓ Contentment: A feeling of peaceful satisfaction with one's current situation or life.
- ✓ Inspiration: A feeling of excitement or motivation brought on by an idea or creative experience.
- ✓ Confidence: A feeling of self-assurance and belief in one's abilities.
- ✓ Happiness: A general feeling of contentment and well-being
- ✓ Love: A strong affectionate attachment to another person
- ✓ Excitement: A feeling of enthusiastic anticipation or eagerness
- ✓ Satisfaction: A sense of contentment or fulfillment from achieving a goal or desire
- ✓ Hope: A positive expectation for the future
- ✓ Amusement: A feeling of lightheartedness and playfulness.

It is important to note that positive emotions can exist in varying degrees, and some may be felt more frequently or intensely than others. Additionally, positive emotions can co-exist with negative emotions and can be experienced in response to different events and experiences.

Overcoming Obstacles to Positive Emotions

Overcoming obstacles to positive emotions is a crucial aspect of cultivating a happier and more fulfilling life. Despite our best efforts to focus on the positive, negative thoughts and emotions can often take over, making it difficult to maintain a positive outlook. However, with the right techniques and mindset, it is possible to overcome these obstacles and cultivate a greater sense of well-being.

Techniques To Cultivate Positive Emotions

- Mindfulness: Practicing mindfulness can help individuals stay present in the moment, leading to increased feelings of peace, happiness, and contentment. This can be achieved through meditation, yoga, or simply taking a few moments to focus on the present moment without judgment.
- Gratitude Practice: Expressing gratitude and appreciation for the positive aspects of one's life can increase feelings of joy and contentment. This can be done by keeping a gratitude journal, writing thank-you letters, or simply taking time to reflect on what one is thankful for.
- Positive Self-Talk: Challenging negative self-talk and replacing it with positive, supportive statements can help improve self-esteem and overall emotional well-being.
- Physical Activity: Engaging in physical activity, such as exercise, yoga, or dance, can release endorphins that improve mood and boost energy levels.
- Social Connections: Spending time with loved ones and building meaningful relationships can increase feelings of happiness, joy, and love.
- Engaging in Hobbies: Pursuing hobbies and interests that bring joy and fulfillment can provide a sense of purpose and help boost overall emotional well-being.

- Acts of Kindness: Performing acts of kindness, such as volunteering or simply helping others, can increase feelings of compassion and happiness.
- Challenging Negative Thoughts: Challenging negative thoughts and reframing them in a more positive light can help improve overall emotional well-being.

It is important to find what works best for each individual, as different techniques may have different levels of effectiveness for different people. Incorporating a combination of techniques and finding what works best can lead to improved emotional health and well-being.

Building Emotional Resilience

Emotional resilience refers to the ability to effectively manage and bounce back from difficult emotions, stress, and adversity. It is the capacity to adapt and thrive in the face of challenges, and is an important aspect of mental and emotional health.

Building emotional resilience involves developing skills and strategies that help individuals to manage their emotions, stress, and challenges in a healthy and adaptive way. Here are some ways to build emotional resilience:

- ✓ Practice self-care: Engage in activities that promote physical and emotional well-being, such as exercise, healthy eating, and sleep.
- ✓ Build strong relationships: Surround yourself with supportive and positive relationships, and engage in meaningful social connections.
- ✓ Develop a growth mindset: Focus on personal growth and development, and approach challenges and failures as opportunities for growth and learning.
- ✓ Engage in stress-reducing activities: Find healthy ways to manage stress, such as exercise, meditation, or journaling.
- ✓ Cultivate a positive outlook: Focus on the positive aspects of life, and adopt a positive and optimistic outlook on challenges and setbacks.
- ✓ Seek support: Don't be afraid to reach out for help when needed. Support from friends, family, or a mental health professional can be incredibly beneficial in building emotional resilience.

Building emotional resilience takes time and effort, but the benefits are well worth it. By developing these skills and strategies, individuals can improve their ability to manage difficult emotions, stress, and adversity, and improve their overall well-being.

Reframing Negative Thoughts

Reframing negative thoughts involves changing the way we think about negative experiences and emotions. It is a cognitive strategy that helps individuals to view their experiences in a more positive and constructive light. Negative thoughts can often be distorted and unhelpful, leading to negative emotions and a vicious cycle of negative thinking. Reframing negative thoughts can help to break this cycle and promote a more positive outlook.

Here are some steps for reframing negative thoughts:

- ✓ Identify negative thoughts: Pay attention to negative thoughts as they occur, and write them down.
- ✓ Challenge the negative thought: Ask yourself if the thought is based in fact or is just a negative perception. Consider alternative perspectives or explanations for the situation.
- ✓ Reframe the thought: Replace the negative thought with a positive or neutral thought. For example, instead of thinking "I'm a failure," reframe the thought to "I may not have succeeded this time, but I can learn from my mistakes and try again."
- ✓ Repeat the new thought: Repeat the reframed thought until it becomes a more automatic and positive way of thinking.

Reframing negative thoughts takes time and practice, but it can be an incredibly effective way to improve mood, reduce stress, and promote overall well-being. By changing the way we think about our experiences, we can change the way we feel and respond to them.

Self-Care And Self-Compassion

Self-care and self-compassion refer to the practice of taking care of one's physical, emotional, and mental well-being. Self-care involves engaging in activities and behaviors that promote health and well-being, while self-compassion involves treating oneself with kindness, understanding, and support, especially during difficult times. Self-care can involve activities such as exercise, healthy eating, sleep, and relaxation, as well as behaviors such as setting boundaries, saying no to commitments that are not a priority, and engaging in hobbies and interests. Self-compassion involves treating oneself with the same kindness, understanding, and support that one would offer to a friend. It involves recognizing and accepting one's own feelings and experiences, and being gentle with oneself rather than self-critical or harsh.

Both self-care and self-compassion are important aspects of emotional and mental well-being, as they help individuals to manage stress, reduce negative emotions, and promote feelings of happiness and contentment. By prioritizing self-care and self-compassion, individuals can build a stronger foundation of emotional resilience and well-being.

Developing A Growth Mindset

A growth mindset is the belief that one's abilities, intelligence, and personality can be developed and improved through hard work, dedication, and effort. This perspective contrasts with a fixed mindset, which views abilities as innate and unchanging.

Developing a growth mindset can have numerous benefits for mental and emotional health, including:

- ✓ Increased motivation: A growth mindset leads to a greater motivation to take on challenges, learn new skills, and persist in the face of setbacks.

- ✓ Improved resilience: Individuals with a growth mindset are better able to bounce back from failure and see it as a valuable learning opportunity.
- ✓ Increased confidence: A growth mindset leads to increased confidence, as individuals feel capable of improving their abilities and achieving their goals.
- ✓ Better mental health: A growth mindset is associated with better mental health outcomes, including reduced anxiety, depression, and stress.

Here are some steps for developing a growth mindset:

- ✓ Embrace challenges: Approach challenges and difficulties as opportunities for growth and learning, rather than as threats or sources of stress.
- ✓ Practice self-reflection: Take time to reflect on your own abilities, strengths, and areas for growth.
- ✓ Cultivate a positive outlook: Focus on the positive aspects of life and adopt an optimistic outlook, even in the face of setbacks and challenges.
- ✓ Seek feedback: Seek feedback from others, and use it as an opportunity to learn and grow.
- ✓ Surround yourself with positive influences: Surround yourself with individuals who support and encourage growth, and avoid those who promote a fixed or negative mindset.

Developing a growth mindset takes time and effort, but the benefits are well worth it. By embracing the belief that abilities can be developed and improved, individuals can improve their mental and emotional well-being and achieve their full potential.

Improving Communication Skills

Improving communication skills is crucial for developing and maintaining healthy relationships, both personal and professional. Good communication involves being able to effectively convey one's thoughts, feelings, and ideas, as well as being able to actively listen and understand others.

Active Listening-Active listening is a communication skill that involves fully focusing on and paying attention to the person who is speaking. It goes beyond just hearing what is being said, and involves actively trying to understand the speaker's message, feelings, and perspectives.

Here are some key components of active listening:

- ✓ Pay attention: Give the speaker your full attention and avoid distractions, such as checking your phone or looking around the room.
- ✓ Show interest: Demonstrate your interest in what the speaker is saying by nodding, making eye contact, and asking clarifying questions.
- ✓ Refrain from interrupting: Allow the speaker to fully express themselves without interrupting or finishing their sentences for them.
- ✓ Paraphrase: Repeat back what you have heard to demonstrate that you understand the speaker's message.
- ✓ Empathize: Try to understand the speaker's perspective and feelings, and show empathy by acknowledging their emotions.

Active listening helps to reduce stress and anxiety, as it promotes a sense of understanding and validation.

Assertiveness Training- Assertiveness training is a type of training or therapy that aims to help individuals develop and improve their assertiveness skills. Assertiveness is the ability to express one's opinions, feelings, and needs in a confident and direct manner, without being aggressive or passive. It involves being able to communicate effectively, set clear boundaries, and handle conflicts in a healthy and effective way. Assertiveness training can take different forms, including group therapy, workshops, coaching sessions, or self-help books and materials. The training typically involves learning about different communication styles, how to recognize and manage one's emotions, and how to express oneself in a way that is respectful and assertive.

This type of training can be beneficial for individuals who struggle with expressing themselves effectively, setting boundaries, or handling conflict. By learning assertiveness skills, individuals can improve their self-esteem, confidence, and relationships with others. Assertiveness training can also help individuals communicate more effectively in both personal and professional settings.

Dealing With Stress

Stress is a normal part of life and is defined as a response to perceived threats, challenges, or demands. When we experience stress, our bodies activate the "fight or flight" response, which prepares us to respond to a perceived danger. This response triggers the release of hormones, such as cortisol and adrenaline, which can cause physical and emotional changes.

However, when stress becomes chronic, it can have negative impacts on emotional health and well-being. Chronic stress can lead to feelings of anxiety, irritability, and depression, and can also contribute to physical health problems, such as headaches, digestive issues, and heart disease. Chronic stress can also weaken the immune system, making individuals more susceptible to illness. In addition to its physical health effects, chronic stress can also have a negative impact on mental health. Stress can exacerbate symptoms of anxiety and depression and can make it difficult for individuals to manage their emotions. Chronic stress can also lead to feelings of burnout, exhaustion, and hopelessness, and can affect relationships, work performance, and overall quality of life.

Therefore, it is important to manage stress in order to maintain emotional health and well-being. This can involve identifying the sources of stress, developing stress management strategies, and seeking support from loved ones, friends, or mental health professionals. Incorporating stress management techniques into daily life can help reduce stress levels, improve emotional health, and promote overall well-being.

Understanding The Causes of Stress and Anxiety

Understanding the causes of stress and anxiety is an important step in managing these emotions and improving one's overall well-being. Stress and anxiety are normal human emotions that everyone experiences from time to time. However, when stress and anxiety become chronic, they can have a negative impact on one's physical and mental health.

There are many factors that can contribute to stress and anxiety, including:

- ✓ Life events: Major changes in life, such as the loss of a job, a death in the family, or a divorce, can lead to stress and anxiety.
- ✓ Work environment: A high-pressure work environment, long hours, and job insecurity can contribute to stress and anxiety.
- ✓ Health problems: Chronic physical or mental health problems can cause stress and anxiety.
- ✓ Financial difficulties: Money problems, debt, and financial uncertainty can contribute to stress and anxiety.

- ✓ Relationship problems: Conflicts with family, friends, or romantic partners can cause stress and anxiety.
- ✓ Personal and psychological factors: Low self-esteem, perfectionism, and negative self-talk can also contribute to stress and anxiety.

It's important to understand that stress and anxiety can have multiple causes and can interact with each other. By identifying the underlying causes of stress and anxiety, individuals can better understand their emotions and take steps to manage them. This can include making changes to one's lifestyle, seeking support from family and friends, and seeking professional help if needed.

Techniques To Manage Stress

Some techniques to manage stress include:

- Exercise: Regular physical activity can help reduce stress levels and improve mood.
- Relaxation techniques: Practicing relaxation techniques, such as deep breathing, progressive muscle relaxation, and yoga, can help calm the mind and body.
- Time management: Prioritizing tasks, setting realistic goals, and learning to say no can help reduce stress levels and improve overall productivity.
- Support systems: Having strong support systems in place, such as friends, family, or support groups, can help individuals manage stress and improve their overall emotional health.
- Hobbies and interests: Engaging in hobbies and interests can help individuals take their minds off of stressors and improve their overall mood.
- Sleep: Getting adequate sleep can help individuals feel refreshed and reduce stress levels.

A mental health professional can help you identify the root causes of stress, develop effective stress management strategies, and improve your overall emotional well-being.

Coping With Anxiety

Anxiety can be overwhelming and debilitating, but there are several effective strategies that can help you cope with it:

- ✓ Practice mindfulness: Mindfulness involves paying attention to the present moment, without judgment. It can help you to focus your mind and reduce racing thoughts. You can try mindfulness meditation, deep breathing exercises, or yoga.
- ✓ Exercise regularly: Regular physical activity has been shown to help reduce anxiety symptoms. Exercise releases endorphins, which can improve your mood and boost self-esteem.
- ✓ Challenge negative thoughts: Try to identify negative thoughts and reframe them in a more positive light. Write down your thoughts and reframe them as affirmations, such as "I am capable and strong."
- ✓ Connect with others: Talking to friends, family, or a mental health professional can help you feel supported and less alone. Joining a support group can also be beneficial.
- ✓ Get enough sleep: Lack of sleep can exacerbate anxiety symptoms. Aim for 7-9 hours of sleep each night.
- ✓ Limit caffeine and alcohol: Both of these substances can increase anxiety symptoms, so it's important to limit your intake.
- ✓ Practice self-care: Engage in activities that bring you joy, such as hobbies or spending time with loved ones. Also, make sure to eat a healthy diet, stay hydrated, and engage in activities that promote relaxation.

Improving Emotional Intelligence

Emotional intelligence (EI) refers to the ability to recognize, understand, and manage one's own emotions, as well as the emotions of others. It encompasses a set of skills and competencies that allow individuals to effectively navigate social situations, build relationships, and make decisions that are in line with their goals and values.

Importance Of Emotional Intelligence In Emotional Health

Emotional intelligence plays a crucial role in emotional health, as it helps individuals develop a better understanding of their own emotions and the emotions of others. This understanding can lead to improved self-awareness and self-regulation, which in turn can lead to a more positive and fulfilling life.

Having high emotional intelligence can help individuals better manage their stress levels, regulate their emotions in challenging situations, and build stronger relationships with others. It can also lead to improved decision making, increased empathy and compassion, and a greater ability to navigate interpersonal conflicts in a constructive and effective way. Moreover, individuals with high emotional intelligence are better equipped to identify and cope with their own negative emotions, such as anger, anxiety, or depression. This can lead to better mental health and a greater sense of well-being. In short, emotional intelligence is an important aspect of emotional health as it enables individuals to understand and manage their emotions in a positive and healthy way, leading to improved relationships, better mental health, and overall well-being.

Emotional intelligence can also lead to greater career success. People with high emotional intelligence are often better able to communicate and work effectively with others, resolve conflicts, and lead teams. These skills can be valuable in the workplace and can lead to promotions and increased job satisfaction. Research has also shown that individuals with high emotional intelligence are more resilient and better able to bounce back from setbacks and challenges. They are also more optimistic and have a more positive outlook on life, which can contribute to better mental health and well-being. However, it's important to note that emotional intelligence is not a fixed trait and can be developed and improved over time. This can be achieved through a variety of methods, such as mindfulness meditation, cognitive-behavioral therapy, or emotional intelligence training programs. Emotional intelligence is a critical component of emotional health and well-being. By improving one's understanding and management of emotions, individuals can experience better relationships, increased job satisfaction, greater resilience, and improved mental health.

Understanding Emotional Intelligence

Emotional Intelligence is a relatively new field of study that has gained increasing attention over the past few decades. It refers to a person's ability to recognize, understand, and manage their own emotions, as well as the emotions of others. It encompasses a set of skills and competencies that help individuals navigate the complex social and emotional landscape of their lives. There are several components of Emotional Intelligence, including self-awareness, empathy, emotion management, and relationship management. Self-awareness involves being aware of one's own emotions and how they affect thoughts, behaviors, and actions. Empathy involves being able to understand the emotions of others and respond in a supportive and understanding manner. Emotion management involves being able to regulate one's own emotions and manage them in a healthy and productive way. And relationship management involves being able to build and maintain positive relationships with others.

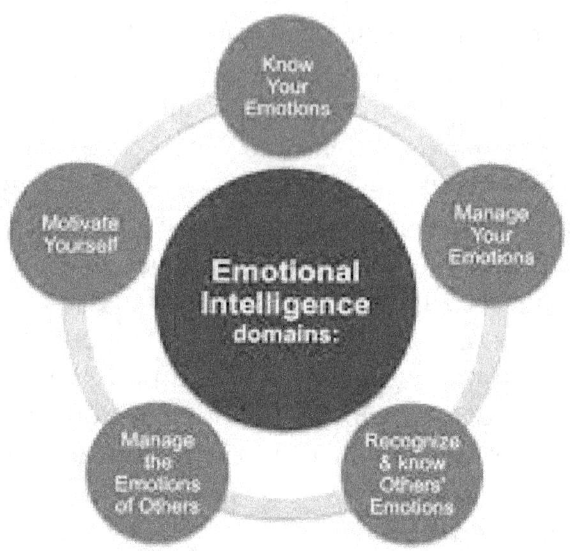

Emotional Intelligence is different from IQ, or cognitive intelligence, which measures a person's ability to solve problems, understand complex concepts, and think abstractly. While IQ is important, Emotional Intelligence is increasingly being recognized as equally important, if not more so, in many areas of life. This is because it plays a critical role in a person's ability to navigate the social and emotional landscape of their life, and has a major impact on relationships, work, and overall well-being.

To develop Emotional Intelligence, individuals can start by becoming more self-aware. This involves paying attention to one's own emotions, recognizing what triggers them, and being mindful of how they affect thoughts, behaviors, and actions. One way to increase self-awareness is through mindfulness practices, such as meditation or journaling. By becoming more aware of one's own emotions, individuals can start to develop a better understanding of their strengths and weaknesses, and work to improve areas where they may be lacking. Another important component of Emotional Intelligence is empathy. Empathy involves being able to understand the emotions of others and respond in a supportive and understanding manner. It requires an individual to put themselves in another person's shoes and see things from their perspective.

To build empathy, individuals can practice active listening, which involves really paying attention to what someone is saying and showing genuine interest in their thoughts and feelings. Emotion management is also a critical component of Emotional Intelligence. This involves being able to regulate one's own emotions and manage them in a healthy and productive way. This can involve identifying negative emotions, such as anger or anxiety, and learning techniques to manage them effectively. For example, taking deep breaths, engaging in physical activity, or seeking support from a friend or therapist can all be effective ways to manage negative emotions. Additionally, cultivating positive emotions, such as gratitude and happiness, can help individuals maintain a more positive outlook and improve their overall emotional well-being.

Finally, relationship management is an important aspect of Emotional Intelligence. This involves being able to build and maintain positive relationships with others. This can involve learning effective communication skills, resolving conflicts in a healthy way, and working effectively as part of a team. By developing strong relationships, individuals can build supportive networks of friends and family, which can help them navigate the ups and downs of life with greater ease.

Emotional Intelligence is a critical component of overall well-being, and individuals who possess high levels of Emotional Intelligence tend to be more successful in all areas of their lives. By developing self-awareness, empathy, emotion management skills, and relationship management skills, individuals can improve their Emotional Intelligence and lead more fulfilling and successful lives.

Components Of Emotional Intelligence

Emotional intelligence (EI) is a type of intelligence that involves the ability to understand and manage one's own emotions and those of others. It is a critical component of success in various aspects of life, such as relationships, work, and personal growth. Emotional intelligence has four key components, which are self-awareness, self-regulation, empathy, and social skills.

Self-awareness is the first component of emotional intelligence, and it involves being aware of one's own emotions and their impact on others. This includes understanding one's strengths, weaknesses, values, and beliefs, as well as being able to recognize and label emotions accurately. People who are self-aware are able to reflect on their own emotions and behavior, and can understand how they affect others.

Self-regulation is the second component of emotional intelligence, and it involves the ability to control and manage one's own emotions. This includes being able to manage impulses, delay gratification, and manage stress effectively. People who are able to regulate their emotions are able to stay calm and composed in challenging situations, and are less likely to engage in impulsive or destructive behavior.

Empathy is the third component of emotional intelligence, and it involves the ability to understand and share the feelings of others. This includes being able to read nonverbal cues, understand emotions, and respond with care and compassion. Empathy helps individuals build strong relationships with others, and it is a critical component of emotional intelligence because it allows individuals to understand the perspectives of others and respond to their emotional needs.

Social skills are the final component of emotional intelligence, and they involve the ability to effectively communicate and interact with others. This includes being able to listen actively, resolve conflicts, and engage in constructive discussions. People with strong social skills are able to build strong relationships with others, and they are able to navigate social situations with ease and grace.

In conclusion, emotional intelligence is a complex and multifaceted construct that involves four key components: self-awareness, self-regulation, empathy, and social skills. These components are critical for success in various aspects of life, such as relationships, work, and personal growth. By developing these components, individuals can improve their emotional intelligence and lead happier, more fulfilling lives.

Techniques To Improve Emotional Intelligence

There are several techniques that can be used to improve emotional intelligence. Here are some of the most effective ones:

Self-reflection: Self-reflection is the process of examining and evaluating one's own thoughts, feelings, and behaviors. It involves taking time to reflect on your experiences and emotions, and considering how they impact your life and the lives of those around you. Self-reflection can help you gain insight into your own emotions, motivations, and values, and can lead to improved self-awareness and emotional intelligence. Self-reflection can take many forms, such as journaling, meditating, or talking to a trusted friend or therapist. The key is to take a step back from your daily experiences and thoughts, and to examine them in a more introspective and analytical way. This process can help you identify patterns in your behavior, understand your triggers and reactions, and gain a deeper understanding of your emotions. Self-reflection can be a powerful tool for personal growth and can lead to greater self-awareness, self-acceptance, and emotional regulation. By taking time to reflect on your experiences, you can gain a better understanding of yourself and develop skills that can help you navigate life's challenges in a more positive and effective way.

Mindfulness: Mindfulness is a mental state achieved by focusing one's awareness on the present moment, while calmly acknowledging and accepting one's thoughts, feelings, and bodily sensations. It involves paying attention to the present moment in a non-judgmental way, and accepting things as they are, rather than trying to control or change them. Mindfulness can be practiced through mindfulness meditation, yoga, or other mindfulness-based activities. It has been shown to have a number of benefits, including reducing stress and anxiety, improving mood, and increasing emotional intelligence.

In terms of emotional intelligence, mindfulness can help individuals become more self-aware and better understand their emotions. By paying attention to their thoughts and feelings in a non-judgmental way, individuals can gain insight into their emotional patterns and reactions, and develop strategies for regulating their emotions. Additionally, mindfulness can also help individuals develop empathy and compassion for others, as they learn to observe their own thoughts and feelings with an open and accepting attitude. Mindfulness is a powerful tool for improving emotional intelligence, as it helps individuals become more self-aware, regulate their emotions, and build stronger relationships with others.

Emotional labeling: Emotional labeling is the process of accurately identifying and labeling one's emotions. This involves recognizing what emotions you are feeling, such as anger, joy, sadness, or frustration, and giving them a name.

Emotional labeling is an important aspect of emotional intelligence because it helps individuals understand their emotions and become more self-aware. By accurately identifying their emotions, individuals can gain insight into their thoughts and behaviors, and learn to regulate their emotions more effectively. In addition, emotional labeling can also improve communication with others. When individuals are able to accurately identify and express their emotions, they can communicate their thoughts and feelings more effectively, leading to improved relationships and reduced conflict. It's important to note that emotional labeling is a skill that can be developed and improved over time. With practice, individuals can become more skilled at recognizing and labeling their emotions, and can use this skill to enhance their emotional intelligence and overall well-being. Emotional labeling is a critical component of emotional intelligence and can lead to greater self-awareness, improved communication, and enhanced emotional regulation. By accurately identifying and labeling your emotions, you can better understand and manage them, leading to a more fulfilling and emotionally healthy life.

Active listening: Active listening is a communication skill that involves paying close attention to what someone is saying, both verbally and non-verbally, and demonstrating that you understand their message. It is a key aspect of emotional intelligence because it helps individuals build stronger relationships with others and improves their ability to understand and respond to the emotions of others.

Active listening involves several key components:

- ✓ Paying attention: Give the speaker your full attention and focus on what they are saying. Avoid distractions such as your phone or other electronic devices.
- ✓ Asking questions: Show that you are engaged and interested in what the speaker is saying by asking clarifying questions.
- ✓ Paraphrasing: Repeat back what the speaker has said in your own words to demonstrate that you understand their message.
- ✓ Non-verbal cues: Pay attention to the speaker's body language, tone of voice, and other non-verbal cues to gain a deeper understanding of their emotions.
- ✓ Avoiding distractions: Avoid interrupting the speaker or being distracted by other things while they are speaking.

By incorporating these components, individuals can improve their active listening skills and become more effective communicators. Additionally, active listening can help individuals build stronger relationships with others, as it demonstrates respect and understanding for the other person's thoughts and feelings. active listening is a critical component of emotional intelligence, and is essential for building strong relationships and improving communication skills. By practicing active listening, individuals can gain a deeper understanding of the emotions and perspectives of others, leading to a more fulfilling and emotionally healthy life.

Empathy: Empathy is the ability to understand and share the feelings of another person. It involves being able to put oneself in someone else's shoes, to feel what they are feeling, and to understand their perspective. Empathy is a key component of emotional intelligence because it helps individuals build strong relationships with others, and improves their ability to understand and respond to the emotions of others.

There are several key elements of empathy, including:

- ✓ Understanding: The ability to understand the thoughts and feelings of another person.
- ✓ Perspective-taking: The ability to see the situation from another person's perspective and understand their emotions.
- ✓ Emotional response: The ability to feel an appropriate emotional response to the emotions of others, such as compassion or sadness.
- ✓ Communication: The ability to communicate understanding and support to the other person in a non-judgmental way.

Empathy is an important aspect of emotional intelligence because it allows individuals to build deeper connections with others and improves their ability to navigate complex social situations. By being empathetic, individuals can improve their relationships, resolve conflicts, and provide support to others in need. Empathy is a critical component of emotional intelligence and is essential for building strong relationships and improving communication skills. By developing empathy, individuals can gain a deeper understanding of the emotions and perspectives of others, leading to a more fulfilling and emotionally healthy life.

Assertiveness: Assertiveness is the ability to express one's thoughts, feelings, and needs in a confident and direct manner, while still respecting the rights and feelings of others. It is an important aspect of emotional intelligence because it allows individuals to effectively communicate their needs and opinions, and to stand up for themselves in situations where their rights or values are being threatened.

Assertiveness involves several key components, including:

- ✓ Self-expression: The ability to express one's thoughts and feelings in a clear and direct manner.
- ✓ Confidence: The ability to express oneself with confidence, without being aggressive or passive.
- ✓ Respect: The ability to express oneself in a way that respects the rights and feelings of others.
- ✓ Boundary-setting: The ability to set and maintain healthy personal boundaries, and to say "no" when necessary.

Assertiveness is an important aspect of emotional intelligence because it allows individuals to effectively communicate their needs and opinions, and to stand up for themselves in situations where their rights or values are being threatened. Additionally, assertiveness can lead to greater self-esteem and improved relationships, as it demonstrates respect for oneself and for others. Assertiveness is a critical component of emotional intelligence, and is essential for building strong relationships and improving communication skills. By developing assertiveness, individuals can gain greater confidence, respect, and the ability to effectively communicate their thoughts and feelings, leading to a more fulfilling and emotionally healthy life.

Conflict resolution: Conflict resolution refers to the process of resolving conflicts or disagreements between individuals or groups. It is an important aspect of emotional intelligence because it allows individuals to effectively manage conflicts in a way that is fair and respectful, and that leads to mutually acceptable outcomes.

Conflict resolution involves several key components, including:

- ✓ Identification: The ability to identify and understand the sources of conflict.
- ✓ Communication: The ability to effectively communicate with the parties involved in the conflict, and to listen to their perspectives.
- ✓ Problem-solving: The ability to collaborate with the parties involved to find mutually acceptable solutions to the conflict.
- ✓ Compromise: The ability to make compromises and negotiate in order to reach a resolution.
- ✓ Empathy: The ability to understand the emotions and perspectives of the parties involved in the conflict.

Conflict resolution is an important aspect of emotional intelligence because it allows individuals to effectively manage conflicts in a way that is fair and respectful, and that leads to mutually acceptable outcomes. By developing conflict resolution skills, individuals can improve their relationships and build stronger, more resilient communities. Conflict resolution is a critical component of emotional intelligence, and is essential for building strong relationships and improving communication skills. By developing conflict resolution skills, individuals can effectively manage conflicts, leading to a more fulfilling and emotionally healthy life.

Emotional expression: Emotional expression refers to the ability to accurately identify, understand, and communicate one's own emotions. It is an important aspect of emotional intelligence because it allows individuals to effectively manage their emotions and to communicate their thoughts and feelings in a clear and meaningful way.

Emotional expression involves several key components, including:

- ✓ Emotional awareness: The ability to accurately identify and understand one's own emotions.
- ✓ Emotional regulation: The ability to effectively manage and control one's emotions.
- ✓ Emotional communication: The ability to communicate one's emotions in a clear and effective manner, using non-verbal cues, tone of voice, and appropriate words.

Emotional expression is important for several reasons. First, it allows individuals to better understand and manage their own emotions, which can lead to greater self-awareness and emotional intelligence. Second, it can improve relationships and communication by allowing individuals to effectively communicate their thoughts and feelings to others. Emotional expression is a critical component of emotional intelligence and is essential for building strong relationships and improving communication skills. By developing emotional expression skills, individuals can gain greater self-awareness and emotional intelligence, leading to a more fulfilling and emotionally healthy life.

Seek feedback: Seeking feedback refers to the practice of actively soliciting opinions and suggestions from others in order to improve one's own performance, behavior, or abilities. It is an important aspect of emotional intelligence because it allows individuals to gain a deeper understanding of their own strengths and weaknesses, and to make necessary changes to improve their personal and professional lives.

Seeking feedback involves several key components, including:

- ✓ Openness: The willingness to listen to and consider the opinions and suggestions of others.
- ✓ Active listening: The ability to truly listen to and understand the feedback being given, without becoming defensive or dismissive.
- ✓ Reflectiveness: The ability to reflect on the feedback received, and to consider its implications for personal growth and improvement.
- ✓ Gratitude: The ability to express gratitude and appreciation for the feedback received, and to acknowledge the efforts of the person providing the feedback.

Seeking feedback is an important aspect of emotional intelligence because it allows individuals to gain a deeper understanding of their own strengths and weaknesses, and to make necessary changes to improve their personal and professional lives. Additionally, seeking feedback can lead to stronger relationships, as it demonstrates a commitment to personal growth and a willingness to listen to others. Seeking feedback is a critical component of emotional intelligence and is essential for personal and professional growth. By actively seeking feedback, individuals can gain a deeper understanding of their own strengths and weaknesses, and can make necessary changes to improve their lives, leading to a more fulfilling and emotionally healthy life.

Continual learning: Continual learning refers to the practice of continuously seeking out new knowledge, skills, and experiences in order to improve one's abilities and understanding. It is an important aspect of emotional intelligence because it allows individuals to remain current and relevant in their personal and professional lives, and to better understand and navigate the world around them.

Continual learning involves several key components, including:

- ✓ Curiosity: The desire to learn and explore new ideas, concepts, and experiences.
- ✓ Open-mindedness: The willingness to consider new perspectives and ways of thinking.
- ✓ Adaptability: The ability to adapt to new situations and continuously improve one's skills and abilities.
- ✓ Reflectiveness: The ability to reflect on one's own learning and to consider its implications for personal growth and improvement.

Continual learning is important for several reasons. First, it allows individuals to remain current and relevant in their personal and professional lives, and to better understand and navigate the world around them. Second, it can lead to greater self-awareness and emotional intelligence, as individuals gain a deeper understanding of their own strengths and weaknesses. Continual learning is a critical component of emotional intelligence and is essential for personal and professional growth. By continuously seeking out new knowledge, skills, and experiences, individuals can remain current and relevant, and can improve their emotional intelligence, leading to a more fulfilling and emotionally healthy life.

By incorporating these techniques into your daily life, you can work on improving your emotional intelligence and develop a better understanding and management of your emotions.

The Importance of Maintaining Emotional Health

The importance of maintaining emotional health cannot be overstated. Emotional health refers to a person's ability to understand, manage, and express their emotions in healthy and adaptive ways. Maintaining emotional health is critical for overall well-being and has a significant impact on many aspects of life, including mental health, relationships, physical health, work performance, and personal satisfaction.

- Mental Health: Emotional health is a crucial component of mental health, and individuals with good emotional health are less likely to experience mental health conditions such as anxiety and depression. Emotional health helps individuals to better understand and manage their emotions, which in turn, reduces the risk of mental health problems. When individuals can identify and manage their emotions in a healthy manner, they are better equipped to cope with stress and other challenges, leading to improved mental well-being.

- Relationships: Good emotional health can enhance relationships by enabling individuals to understand and manage their emotions, as well as the emotions of others. This improved emotional intelligence can lead to better communication, stronger relationships, and reduced conflict. By understanding the emotions of others, individuals can build stronger relationships based on empathy, understanding, and mutual respect.

- Physical Health: The link between emotional health and physical health is well-established, and good emotional health can have a positive impact on physical health outcomes such as cardiovascular health, immune system function, and sleep quality. Research has shown that individuals with good emotional health have a reduced risk of physical health problems and are better able to manage existing conditions.

- Work Performance: Good emotional health can improve work performance by enabling individuals to better manage stress and work more effectively in teams. Individuals with strong emotional intelligence are better equipped to build strong relationships with colleagues, deal with conflicts in a healthy manner, and communicate effectively with team members. These skills can lead to increased job satisfaction, improved productivity, and better overall performance at work.

- Personal Satisfaction: Maintaining emotional health can lead to increased personal satisfaction and happiness. When individuals are able to understand and manage their emotions, they are better equipped to deal with life's challenges and enjoy fulfilling relationships. Good emotional health also helps individuals to develop resilience and a positive outlook on life, leading to increased satisfaction and happiness.

- However, maintaining emotional health is a lifelong process that requires ongoing effort and attention. It is essential to develop self-awareness and emotional intelligence, and to incorporate healthy emotional practices into daily life. Some of the techniques that can help maintain emotional health include:

- Self-Reflection: Regular self-reflection is essential for understanding and managing emotions. Take time each day to reflect on your emotions, thoughts, and experiences, and to identify patterns in your emotional responses. This can help you gain insight into your emotional triggers and develop strategies for managing your emotions.

- Empathy: Empathy is the ability to understand and share the feelings of others. By practicing empathy, individuals can build stronger relationships and reduce conflict.

When individuals take the time to understand the emotions of others, they can improve communication and build stronger relationships.

- Active Listening: Active listening is an essential skill for managing emotions. When individuals take the time to listen actively to others, they can better understand their emotions and perspectives, leading to improved relationships and reduced conflict.
- Emotional Regulation: Emotional regulation refers to the ability to manage emotions in healthy and adaptive ways. Techniques such as deep breathing, mindfulness, and cognitive restructuring can help individuals regulate their emotions and manage stress.
- Exercise: Exercise is a great way to improve emotional health and manage stress. Exercise can release endorphins, which are natural mood-boosters, and can also reduce feelings of anxiety and depression.

Overview On How to Become the Boss of Your Emotions

Becoming the boss of your emotions is a process that requires patience, persistence, and dedication. Emotions are a normal and natural part of being human, but when they become intense and overwhelming, they can affect our daily lives and cause problems in our relationships and work. Understanding how to regulate and manage our emotions can help us lead happier, healthier, and more fulfilling lives.

Understanding your emotions

The first step in becoming the boss of your emotions is to understand them. This means recognizing what emotions you are feeling and why. Try to identify patterns in your emotions and the triggers that set them off. This self-awareness will help you understand your emotional responses better and enable you to manage them more effectively.

Accepting your emotions

Once you understand your emotions, it is important to accept them. Emotions, both positive and negative, are a normal part of life and cannot be avoided. Trying to suppress or ignore emotions can lead to bottled-up feelings that can cause harm later on. Instead, try to embrace your emotions and acknowledge them for what they are. This will help you to process and manage them better.

Practicing mindfulness

Mindfulness is a technique that helps you focus on the present moment and become more aware of your thoughts and emotions. Practicing mindfulness can help you to become more attuned to your emotions, allowing you to regulate them more effectively. There are many ways to practice mindfulness, including meditation, deep breathing exercises, and yoga.

Using positive self-talk

Positive self-talk is a powerful tool for managing emotions. When we have negative thoughts, they can intensify our emotions, making them harder to manage. Positive self-talk can help to reframe these thoughts and put them into perspective, making it easier to regulate our emotions. Try to focus on the positive aspects of a situation, and replace negative thoughts with more positive ones.

Developing coping mechanisms

Developing healthy coping mechanisms can help you to manage your emotions in difficult situations. These can include activities like exercise, journaling, or spending time with loved ones. When you have established coping mechanisms, you can turn to them when you feel overwhelmed, helping you to regulate your emotions and reduce stress.

Seeking professional help

If you find that your emotions are affecting your daily life and causing problems, it may be helpful to seek professional help. A mental health professional can provide you with tools and techniques to help you manage your emotions, as well as offer support and guidance.

Living a healthy lifestyle

Living a healthy lifestyle can have a positive impact on your emotions. This includes eating a healthy diet, getting regular exercise, and getting enough sleep. When we take care of our physical health, we are better equipped to manage our emotions and maintain a positive outlook.

In conclusion, becoming the boss of your emotions requires effort, patience, and dedication. By understanding your emotions, accepting them, practicing mindfulness, using positive self-talk, developing coping mechanisms, seeking professional help, and living a healthy lifestyle, you can learn to regulate and manage your emotions, leading a happier and more fulfilling life. Remember, managing emotions is a lifelong journey, and it is important to be kind to yourself and give yourself credit for progress, no matter how small.

Encouragement To Continue the Journey of Being the Boss of Your Emotions

Managing your emotions can be a challenging journey, but it is also a rewarding one. It requires patience, persistence, and dedication, but the benefits of becoming the boss of your emotions are numerous. From improving your relationships to reducing stress and anxiety, the benefits are well worth the effort. If you have started the journey of managing your emotions, but are feeling discouraged, here are some words of encouragement to help you continue on your journey.

Celebrate Small Victories

Managing your emotions is a long-term journey, and progress may be slow at times. However, it is important to celebrate small victories along the way. Whether it is noticing an improvement in your mood or successfully managing a difficult situation, take the time to acknowledge your progress and give yourself credit for the steps you have taken.

Be kind to yourself

It is easy to be hard on yourself when you don't see the progress you want, but it is important to be kind to yourself. Emotional regulation is a complex process and setbacks are normal. If you slip up, don't beat yourself up. Instead, try to learn from the experience and move forward with a positive attitude.

Surround yourself with positive people

Having a support system can make a big difference in your emotional journey. Surround yourself with positive people who are supportive and encouraging. Seek out people who understand what you are going through and can offer guidance and support. Having a network of supportive individuals can help you stay motivated and on track.

Stay committed

Managing your emotions is a lifelong journey, and it requires commitment. When you feel discouraged, remind yourself why you started the journey in the first place and focus on your goals. Remember that progress takes time, and it is important to stay committed to your goals, even when the journey is difficult.

Practice self-care

Self-care is a critical component of emotional regulation. It is important to take care of yourself, both physically and mentally. Engage in activities that bring you joy, whether it is exercise, reading, or spending time with loved ones. Make self-care a priority, and don't be afraid to take a break when you need it.

Seek professional help if necessary

If you are feeling overwhelmed or are having difficulty managing your emotions, it may be helpful to seek professional help. A mental health professional can provide you with tools and techniques to help you manage your emotions, as well as offer support and guidance. Remember, seeking help is a sign of strength, not weakness.

Remember that setbacks are normal

Setbacks are a normal part of any journey, and your emotional journey is no exception. Don't be discouraged when you experience setbacks. Instead, use them as an opportunity to learn and grow. Remember, progress takes time, and setbacks are a natural part of the process.

managing your emotions can be a challenging journey, but it is also a rewarding one. When you feel discouraged, remember to celebrate small victories, be kind to yourself, surround yourself with positive people, stay committed, practice self-care, seek professional help if necessary, and remember that setbacks are normal. Emotional regulation is a lifelong journey, and the rewards of becoming the boss of your emotions are numerous. Stay positive and keep moving forward and you will see progress in your emotional journey.

Conclusion

In conclusion, becoming the boss of your emotions is a critical aspect of maintaining great mental health. By managing your emotions effectively, you can reduce stress, improve your relationships, and increase your overall sense of well-being. The journey to becoming the boss of your emotions is a lifelong process that requires patience, persistence, and dedication, but the benefits are well worth the effort.

To recap, some of the key steps to becoming the boss of your emotions include:

- Understanding your emotions - Knowing your emotions and how they affect your thoughts and behaviors is the first step in managing them effectively.
- Practice self-awareness - Paying attention to your thoughts and emotions in the moment and identifying triggers that cause negative emotions can help you better understand your emotional landscape.
- Practice mindfulness - Mindfulness is a powerful tool that can help you stay present and reduce negative emotions.
- Engage in physical activity - Exercise and physical activity can help release stress, increase positive emotions, and improve your overall mood.
- Engage in self-care - Taking care of your physical and mental health is an important aspect of emotional regulation.
- Seek professional help - If you are struggling to manage your emotions, seeking professional help is a sign of strength, not weakness.
- Practice emotional regulation techniques - There are many techniques that can help you regulate your emotions, including deep breathing, visualization, and cognitive restructuring.

Becoming the boss of your emotions is not an overnight process. It requires patience, persistence, and dedication, but with the right approach and mindset, anyone can do it. Remember, you are in control of your emotions, and with practice and patience, you can become the boss of your emotions.

In summary, becoming the boss of your emotions is an important aspect of great mental health. By taking control of your emotions and learning how to manage them effectively, you can reduce stress, improve your relationships, and increase your overall sense of well-being. So take the time to understand your emotions, practice self-awareness, engage in physical activity, engage in self-care, seek professional help if necessary, and practice emotional regulation techniques. With dedication and patience, you too can become the boss of your emotions.